Mary-Cabrini Durkin ■ ■ ■

The Cathedral of Christ the Light
[Oakland ‖ California]

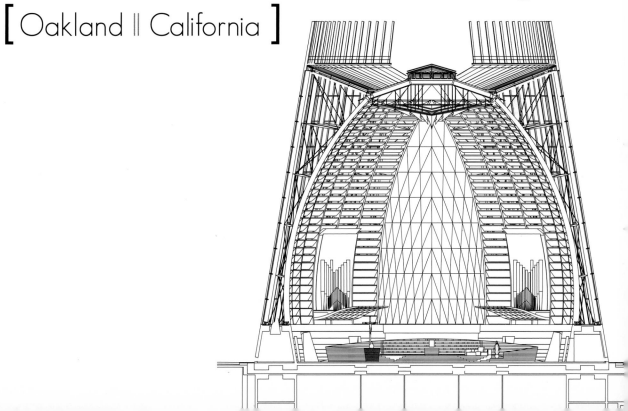

[Credits

Cathedral Photography
Pp. 1-56: John Blaustein

Cathedral Renderings
Skidmore, Owings & Merrill, LLP

Historical Images
• Cathedral of Christ the Light
• *The Catholic Voice*
• Diocese of Oakland
• Archives of the Archdiocese
  of San Francisco
• Holy Names University

Director of Communication
Michael Brown

Consultant
Rev. Paul D. Minnihan, Provost

Historical Resources
• Carmen Batiza
• Paul Bailey Gates
• Jeffrey M. Burns, and Carmen
  Batiza. *We Are the Church:
  A History of the Diocese
  of Oakland.* Oakland:
  Éditions du Signe, 2001.

Publisher
Éditions du Signe - B.P. 94
F-67038 Strasbourg Cedex 2
France
Tel (33) 03 88 78 91 91
Fax (33) 03 88 78 91 99

Publishing Director
Christian Riehl

Director of Publication
Joëlle Bernhard

Publishing Assistant
Anne-Lise Hauchard

Layout
Editions du Signe - 107920

(c) Éditions du Signe, 2008
ISBN 978-2-7468-2067-8

Table of
Contents

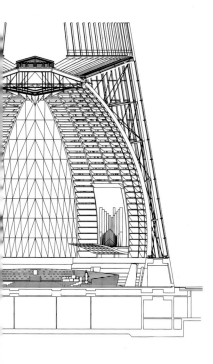

Photo by Gerald Ratto

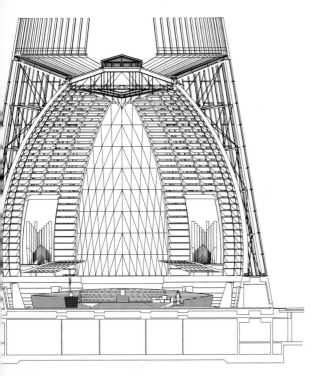

Introduction

What is a cathedral? What is this cathedral?

The Cathedral of Christ the Light is the mother church and home of all the members of the Catholic Church in the Diocese of Oakland. Here they pray together, in a union of spirit that binds them as one body in Christ. In the cathedral, the symbolic center of the diocese, the bishop teaches and leads the Catholic community of Alameda and Contra Costa counties.

The Cathedral of Christ the Light is a proclamation of Christian faith. It speaks in concrete, wood, glass and, above all, in light. The Church continues the mission of Jesus Christ to manifest God in the world.

The Cathedral of Christ the Light is a sacred space, designed and built to illuminate, inspire and ennoble the human spirit. It invites all who come seeking the beauty that opens hearts to goodness and truth. The entire civic community, people of all beliefs, can find a welcome here.

Blending ancient faith, centuries-old architectural elements, and contemporary technology, the cathedral speaks for the ages and for today.

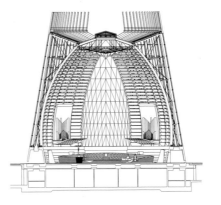

A Vision of
Light

Unique and contemporary, traditional and time-less – Oakland's Cathedral of Christ the Light rises out of the earth on a massive base and dissolves into the heavens. Fusing such polar elements, the cathedral speaks a universal human language. The Word that it speaks is "Christ."

"Let there be light!"

. . . .

Architecture makes a statement. Here it is a proclamation: Jesus Christ is the Light of All Nations. The cathedral's builders planned and designed and constructed for this purpose. From the early days of diocesan consultation, this intention guided the process: to manifest the faith that Christ is the meaning and the goal of Creation. The cathedral expresses this belief primarily in terms of light. It teaches its very meaning through its beauty.

The Book of Genesis places light at the very beginning: "Let there be light!" Instinct itself draws humanity toward light. Churches traditionally use light as a metaphor for God's grace and presence. Oakland's cathedral expresses a vision that is both elemental and complex.

Architect Craig Hartman sought to create a space of "ephemeral lightness" with a "primordial connection to the earth." He and his colleagues at Skidmore, Owings & Merrill, LLP, used natural materials such as wood and the glass (formed by sand and fire) and concrete (sand and water) developed by ancient Roman • • •

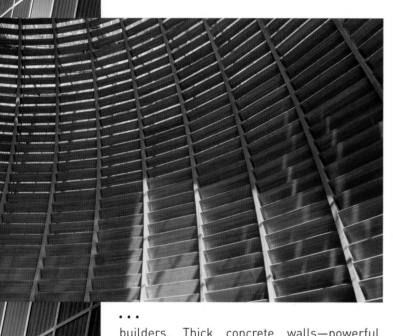

• • •

builders. Thick concrete walls—powerful, solid—situate the cathedral firmly on the earth. Douglas fir ribs create a vault that suggests a forest opening to the sky. Exterior glass panels, textured by baked-in ceramic frits, filter the light. A coat of laminate between the two layers of glass creates a subtle luminosity as light passes through it.

Entering, one is lifted heavenward.

Light does not simply illuminate this cathedral. It is intrinsic to it. The building creates an experience of light, a fluid, ever-changing experience. Through the turning seasons, the sun's rays strike it differently each day, and in each hour of the day. With a brilliant sun or a cloudy day—the cathedral feels different. At times the outside world is subtly visible.

Experiencing the cathedral from outside also offers varied and meaningful perspectives. For example, the architect described different phenomena of light on the glass exterior: "When the light is strongest on the surface facing the viewer, the veil will appear opaque. When it is strongest behind the viewing surface, it will appear to glow. In the fog or in flat light, the glass will seem to dissolve." Under some conditions, the rare view of sunlight striking an opposite inner wall can be seen from the plaza.

The cathedral also speaks to and teaches those who see it from outside, even from afar. Lighted from within, at night it glows. The building itself is an icon of Christ for the city, as the Book of Revelation declares, "The glory of God gave it light, and its lamp was the Lamb" (Revelation 21:23). Christ is the Lamb. Christ is the light shining in the darkness (John 1:5), a beacon drawing humanity to God. The Christian's mission is to share that light with the world.

A place of light—a place of grace—a place of God's creative energy and saving love—Christ, the Light of the World.

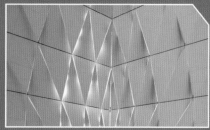
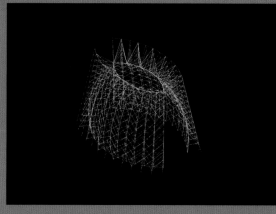

Craig W. Hartman,
FAIA

Light as a sacred phenomenon, manifesting God's presence—that was the principle guiding architect Craig W. Hartman in designing Oakland's cathedral.

As a twenty-year-old architecture student, Hartman had life-altering encounters with light in two French churches. Medieval stained glass dazzled him with color in Sainte-Chapelle in Paris. In the Chapel of Notre Dame du Haut in Ronchamp, he felt the mystery of filtered light in the work of twentieth-century architect Le Corbusier.

With a bachelor's degree from Ball State University, Indiana, Hartman was selected for advanced studies at the Architecture Association in London. His career has involved academic contributions at many other universities.

As design partner for Skidmore, Owings & Merrill, LLP, he has designed buildings of many types, urban districts and even furnishings, all in a contemporary style that respects place as well as function. His recent works in San Francisco have included the International Terminal at the airport, the St. Regis Museum Tower, and affordable housing in the Tenderloin district. His designs are in Europe and Asia as well as in the United States; the American embassy in Beijing is his design.

The American Institute of Architects elected Hartman to the College of Fellows in 1995 for his contributions in the field of architectural design. The youngest recipient of the Maybeck Award, he was recognized by the AIA California chapter in 2001 for "lifetime achievement."

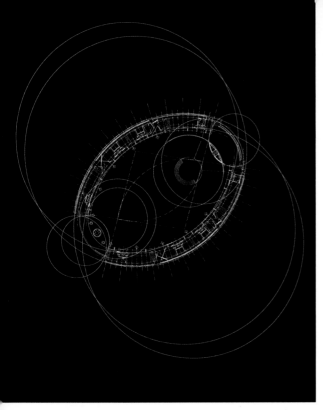

Architect Craig Hartman and his team at Skidmore, Owings & Merrill began with the "*vesica pisces*" (also termed "*vesica piscis*") form shown in this computer rendering: two overlapping circles with a shared radius.

"Sacred" Geometry

Geometric patterns tease and please the eye. They also frame the building's meaning. The lines and curves shape a vault with sacred meaning. In this way, too, the cathedral speaks of Christ.

The outer walls are conical segments. If carried to its apex, the cone would close.

Instead, however, it opens to the sky, to the heavenly vault that continues upward into infinity.

The spherical contours of the inner walls represent intersecting circles. As a result, the space within has the shape of a fish, called "*vesica pisces*" (also termed "*vesica piscis*").

Intriguing geometric and mathematical applications of this shape connect it with patterns in nature and suggest the order of the universe itself. The mathematical proportions represented in the overlapping circles are basic to architectural triumphs such as the Egyptian pyramids, the Parthenon in Athens, the Taj Mahal, and the cathedral of Notre Dame in Paris, among many. The *vesica pisces* image itself was often incorporated into medieval cathedrals.

This form has multi-layered ancient symbolism. Representing an element of the Ark of the Covenant, it connotes the place where God abided among the Israelites on their trek through the desert (in Exodus) and within the Holy of Holies in the Temple of Jerusalem.

The *vesica pisces* served as the first visual symbol of Jesus Christ. Persecuted early Christians used it as a code, based on the word *ICHTHYS* (Greek for fish), an anagram of the Greek words for "Jesus Christ, Son of God and Savior."

Furthermore, this *vesica pisces* shape recalls the Gospel stories in which fish represent the Christian community, drawn into the fisherman Peter's boat, the Church. Eucharistic overtones fill accounts of Jesus multiplying loaves and fish to feed the throng and cooking fish on the seashore to feed the disciples. The risen Christ continues to feed his followers with his word and his Body in every Eucharistic celebration.

The cathedral's curved wooden beams suggest the ribs of a boat and illustrate the traditional name "nave" for the body of a church (from Latin *navis*, meaning "boat" or "ship"). The Book of Genesis offers the image of the Ark, in which God's initiative, with human cooperation, saves humanity from the results of sin, as Noah and his family survive the Great Flood.

This dual architectural theme of both fish and boat is a subtle reminder of the connection between this cathedral and the Pacific Ocean.

Of Earth and Heaven

Simple, natural materials shape this sacred space. Concrete gives it strength. Wood warms it. Glass opens it. In a poetic fusion, light transforms concrete, wood, and glass. Shadows modulate the light with softness and texture. This is a space like none other. Emerging from earth, the cathedral opens to heaven.

This model demonstrates the cathedral's complex dual vaulting. Douglas fir ribs and horizontal louvers form the inner vault. Glass panels set into Douglas fir mullions compose the outer vault, which the architect describes as a "glass veil."

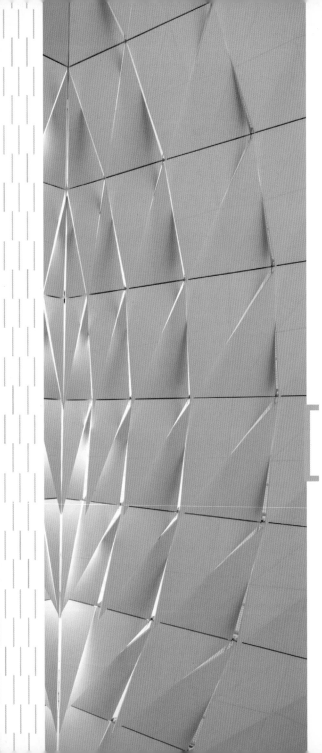

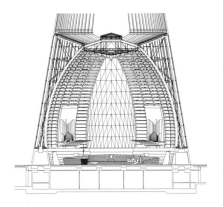

The Diocese of
Oakland

Missionary Origins

The young Diocese of Oakland stands on more than two centuries of Catholic history. Mass was first offered here on March 27, 1772, at the edge of a tidal swamp—now Lake

○ The Mission of San Jose, established in 1797, was the first center of Catholicism in the Oakland area. The church building was restored in 1985.

Merritt—on what is now the site of Our Lady of Lourdes Church. Franciscan Father Francisco de Lasuen, second president of the California missions, founded Mission San Jose on June 11, 1797, in the East Bay area called Oroysom in the local Ohlone language.

Within five years, over 400 hunter-gatherers had joined the agricultural mission settlement. Spanish and native cultures and skills meshed with rich results in religious art and liturgical music. By 1831 the community numbered nearly 1,900. It suffered from many European diseases to which the local people lacked immunity.

Conflict between native peoples and the Spanish military reflected colonial tensions. Missionaries championed their neophytes' rights and retained land for them until a newly independent Mexico secularized the missions in 1833. With the close of Mission San Jose in 1838, the community was dispossessed and dispersed.

The Archdiocese of San Francisco

Most Reverend Joseph Sadoc Alemany, OP (d. 1884), was the first Archbishop of San Francisco.

In 1840 the Diocese of Both Californias was established, with Francisco Garcia Diego y Moreno as bishop. After the war between the United States and Mexico, Upper California found itself a US territory in 1848, a state in 1850. The new Diocese of Monterey became the Archdiocese of San Francisco in 1853, with Joseph Sadoc Alemany, OP, as its first bishop.

After the Gold Rush, the East Bay remained sparsely populated and rural until the Central Pacific Railroad made it the western terminus of the transcontinental rail line in 1868. Population boomed, reaching 35,000 by 1880. It boomed again, with refugees from San Francisco, after the earthquake and fire of 1906.

Parishes multiplied in Oakland and throughout the East Bay. Besides migrants from the East, they served successive waves of immigrants, largely Irish, Portuguese, German, and Italian, mostly in "national" parishes.

Shipbuilding and other industries related to the Second World War created an employment boom that drew many African Americans from the South. Catholics among them initially centered at St. Patrick, St. Joseph, St. Columba and St. Louis Bertrand parishes. Father Clarence Howard, SVD, exercised strong leadership in the African-American Catholic community and in the diocese at large. St. Francis de Sales Cathedral's liturgies would later benefit from

Father Clarence Howard, SVD (left), greets parishioners of St. Patrick Parish. (Photo: Courtesy of *The Catholic Voice*)

the spirituality of African-American Catholics.

The wartime "bracero" labor program drew Mexicans too. Increased awareness of Spanish-speaking workers, including migrants, led Father Charles Phillips and three other priests to form the Spanish Mission Band. Their ministry raised consciousness about social justice. Latino Catholics, then and now a large percentage of the diocese, underline California's historic ties with Hispanic cultures and language. Their vivid devotional life finds its apex in honoring Our Lady of Guadalupe.

The post-war demographic explosion multiplied East Bay parishes and schools. By the 1960s, Alameda and Contra Costa counties counted seventy-five parishes.

Even before its founding, the future Diocese of Oakland had been developing into a microcosm of the nation's latest immigrant experience. New immigrants have flowed in from Mexico and from Central and South America in increasing numbers. The latest waves of new populations link the area ever more closely with the Pacific Basin and Asia: the Philippines, Vietnam, China, Korea, and Laos.

Eritrean-American worshipers recite the Our Father during the 2007 Chautauqua, as the Oakland diocese celebrates its diversity at St. Stephen's Parish in Walnut Creek. (Photo by Greg Tarczynski)

Today, enrichment and challenges mark a multi-cultural, multi-ethnic local Church, 25% immigrant. Sunday Mass is offered in seventeen languages. The diocese welcomes and celebrates its new diversity, for example in an annual "Chautauqua" festival of prayer and song, food and dance and art.

A Vatican II Diocese

Just before the Second Vatican Council, Pope John XXIII divided the Archdiocese of San Francisco, spinning off the new dioceses of Santa Rosa, Stockton, and Oakland on January 13, 1962. Bishop Floyd L. Begin laid the foundations of his East Bay diocese in the spirit of the Council. His commitment to education and to ecumenism included inter-religious collaborative efforts such as the Graduate Theological Union in Berkeley.

 The Most Reverend Floyd Begin was the first bishop of Oakland. (Photo: Courtesy of *The Catholic Voice*)

The Cathedral of St. Francis de Sales

The Holy See designated St. Francis de Sales Church as the original cathedral of the diocese. Bishop Begin declared that he would leave to his successor the task of building a new one. St. Francis de Sales was remodeled to accommodate the liturgical renewal called for by the Second Vatican Council, with the altar facing the people and devotional elements minimized to focus on the eucharistic liturgy.

Under the leadership of Father E. Donald Osuna and Father James Keeley, the cathedral's liturgy became a model of renewal. Drawing on multiple talents and integrating diverse cultural and aesthetic elements, the dynamic liturgies drew worshipers from around the area and formed a laboratory for creativity. The effects rippled across the nation.

Bishop John S. Cummins succeeded the deceased Bishop Begin in 1977. His hopeful spirit continued the legacy of the Second Vatican Council, with wider inclusion of all the baptized in more areas of Church life and governance.

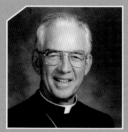

Most Reverend
John S. Cummins

Initiating the process that has led to the Cathedral of Christ the Light, Bishop John S. Cummins sees the cathedral as continuing the teaching mission of Jesus Christ: the message "that each person is worthy of God's love."

Oakland native John Stephen Cummins began his studies for the priesthood at St. Joseph College, a minor seminary, and completed them at San Francisco's St. Patrick Seminary. After ordination in 1953, he combined pastoral and campus ministries in San Francisco and eventually taught at Bishop O'Dowd High School in Oakland.

Bishop Floyd Begin appointed Father Cummins the first diocesan chancellor in 1962. In 1971 he became the executive director of the California Catholic Conference of Bishops and in 1974 Auxiliary Bishop of Sacramento.

Oakland rejoiced to welcome this native son home as its second bishop in 1977. He led with a commitment to inclusion and openness, and with support for social justice.

Bishop Cummins retired in 2003. However, as the episcopal vicar for the cathedral project, he continues to exercise leadership. He rejoices that the cathedral makes Christ's light visible amid a "diverse and united People of God."

<O> Father Donald Osuna (left) leads the choir of the Cathedral of St. Francis de Sales. (Photo: Courtesy of *The Catholic Voice*)

Loma Prieta

Then the earth shook.

Cheering the As, before their third game of the World Series with the San Francisco Giants, Oakland was thinking baseball. On October 17, 1989, the city's attention made a seismic shift. When that evening's 7.1 Loma Prieta quake was over, local Catholics joined in the relief efforts. Then they realized a double loss: both the Cathedral of St. Francis de Sales and Sacred Heart Church had been damaged and were not

usable. Displaced diocesan functions such as Confirmations and Ordinations took place at different parishes, scattered about the diocese. Bishop Cummins accepted reluctantly the reality that St. Francis de Sales could not be used safely. It was razed in October 1993.

The cathedral parish merged with St. Mary's Immaculate Conception in 1993. They were inner-city neighbors, and both had earlier responded to Bishop Begin's charge "to alleviate the problems of the poor, especially those of minority groups."

But the diocese needed a shared home, a place to celebrate together and to experience its unity amid diversity. Bishop Cummins asked the question: Should he undertake a new construction? The foresight and generosity of Oakland philanthropist Gladys Valley helped him make the decision. "Go for it!" she urged.

The Holy Names Group

In late 1999 the bishop gathered representatives from the entire diocese. In three sessions, 103 lay people and 40 priests and religious convened at Holy Names College. On February 17, 2000, the "Holy Names Group" expressed their consensus that planning for a new cathedral (and for additional facilities

supporting the diocesan mission) should proceed. "Now is the time," they said, calling for "a sign of unity among peoples."

A naming subcommittee solicited suggestions and then recommended "Christ the Light." The name recalled the Second Vatican Council, which had so shaped the diocese's beginnings. In a major teaching, *Lumen Gentium* (Light of Nations), the Council spoke of the entire Church's mission to make the Light that is Christ shine among the nations. In the words of Father Osuna, the cathedral seeks to be like a lampstand providing light "for all who seek a home, and for those who may be lost, a beacon in the night."

A Site
. . . .

A fund-raising feasibility study encouraged Bishop Cummins to move forward and appoint leadership. He hired Brother Mel Anderson, FSC, as project director and asked third-generation East Bay native and Oakland lawyer John L. McDonnell, Jr., to chair the steering committee. Suitable sites were explored, and the choice fell upon the southwest corner of Grand Avenue and Harrison Street, occupied by a parking lot. The city had approved an office building for this land but was open to the cathedral proposal. Integrated into Oakland's

The former campus of Holy Names College was a prominent feature along Lake Merritt, on the site now occupied by the Kaiser Center.

downtown, the location affords a vista over Lake Merritt to Adams Point and beyond. The 2.5 acres were purchased in December 2003.

The spot's history reprises significant elements of Oakland's past. Part of the 1820 land grant to Spanish soldier Luis Maria Peralta, it still had a rural atmosphere when the Sisters of the Holy Names of Jesus and Mary settled in 1868. Their 6.5 acres adjoined the present cathedral location. Their neighbor was Central Pacific Railroad baron Albion Harmon, whose estate was later subdivided. For decades, apartment buildings and a series of car dealerships occupied properties facing Lake Merritt and the Children's Fairyland on Adams Point. Holy Names College relocated in 1957, and Henry Kaiser purchased its land for the present Kaiser Center.

The cathedral rises in view of the Kaiser Center, seen behind it.

Lake Merritt is seen from Holy Names College, which once stood on the site now occupied by the Kaiser Center.

The view from the cathedral plaza includes Adams Point, a peninsula in Lake Merritt.

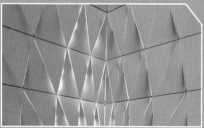

Most Reverend
Allen H. Vigneron

A native of Michigan, Bishop Allen Vigneron studied for the priesthood at Sacred Heart Seminary in Detroit and at the Pontifical Gregorian University in Rome. He earned bachelor's degrees in Arts and in Theology.

Ordained for the Archdiocese of Detroit (1975), he became an associate pastor. He earned a Licentiate in Sacred Theology in 1977 from the Gregorian and then returned to parish ministry. From the Catholic University of America, he earned a master's degree (1983) and a doctorate in philosophy (1987).

First a teacher, then dean (1988) of Sacred Heart College Seminary, he helped develop its graduate theological program. After serving in the Vatican Secretariat of State and teaching at the Gregorian, he was appointed president of Sacred Heart Major Seminary in 1994.

In 1996 he was ordained Auxiliary Bishop of Detroit.

Bishop Vigneron has served on committees of the national bishops' conference and on the boards of several institutions of higher education.

Bishop Vigneron was named Coadjutor Bishop of Oakland in January 2003 and succeeded Bishop Cummins in October of that year. He brought the cathedral from vision to reality: articulating its theology and spirituality, raising funds, empowering skilled leaders, and developing its civic outreach. It was he who introduced the key image of Christ in majesty.

He sees the cathedral's mission as flowing from that of the Church, expressed in *Lumen Gentium*: to be "a sacrament—a sign and instrument . . . of intimate union with God and of the unity of the whole human race."

Gathering Good Together

Bishop Allen H. Vigneron, Oakland's third bishop, took up the torch in 2003, upon Bishop Cummins' retirement. He accepted the challenge of working to raise the necessary funds through private donations, so as not to jeopardize the diocesan budget or services for the poor. Bishop Vigneron created an independent non-profit organization to handle the separate funding and direct the construction. He appointed Bishop Cummins as episcopal vicar for the project and called on business and philanthropic leaders like Jack Smith and John Cecconi, general campaign co-chairs; and Ron Courtney, Molly M. Crowley, and Tom Seeno, regional chairs.

Their efforts, in collaboration with a phalanx of volunteers, generated wide support from individuals, foundations, and corporate and business donors. Memorializing Gladys Valley's earlier advice to Bishop Cummins to proceed with the project, the Wayne and Gladys Valley Foundation made an extremely generous lead gift. All diocesan parishioners had an opportunity to contribute just before the dedication.

This wide support brought to life the hope and commitment for the cathedral's future role in the community: to "Gather Good Together."

The generosity of the cathedral's benefactors is recognized in the Hall of Honor near the cathedral conference center. A restored mosaic from St. Francis de Sales Cathedral (detail at right) is mounted here.

An architectural competition led to the selection of a design by Craig Hartman, FAIA, of Skidmore, Owings & Merrill, in 2003. Brother Mel retired during this period, and Bishop Cummins asked John McDonnell to leave his volunteer status and become overall director of the Cathedral project. McDonnell, while practicing law full-time, had pursued his musical avocation as choir director at the previous cathedral. He was an advisor during Bishop Cummins' planning cycle.

The firm Conversion Management Associates was brought on board in November 2002 to represent the diocese's day-to-day construction management interests. Brother William Woeger, FSC, was hired as liturgical designer.

The Oakland Planning Commission approved the design unanimously in October 2004. Before construction began, with plans incomplete, the projected cost for the full complex was $131 million. Three years later, in order to incorporate projected construction costs and all other project costs, the budget was revised to $190 million.

Bishop Vigneron blessed the land on May 23, 2004. Before ground was broken on May 21, 2005, the name of each parish in the diocese was placed on the surface, signifying that the cathedral would be the home of all.

A woman carrying a bowl of incense, followed by a group of Korean dancers, leads a procession along Lake Merritt to the site of the cathedral groundbreaking on May 21, 2005. (Photo by Greg Tarczynski)

The renowned St. Columba's Praise Dancers perform before the formal groundbreaking ceremony.
(Photo by Greg Tarczynski)

Bishop Allen H. Vigneron
(left), and Bishop Emeritus
John Cummins break ground
for the new cathedral.
(Photo by Greg Tarczynski)

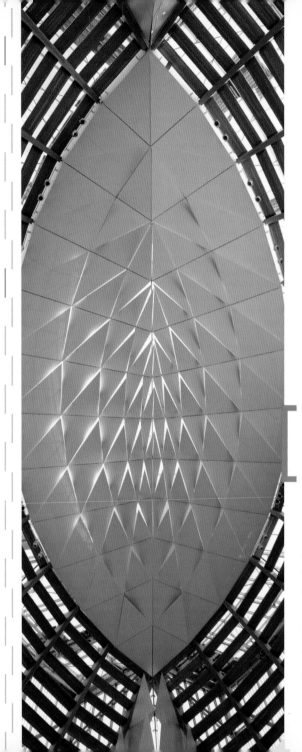

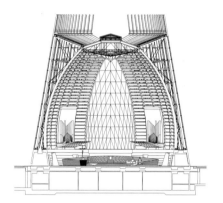

Building a
Cathedral

■ ■ ■

Collaborating closely with Skidmore, Owings
& Merrill, the general contractor, Webcor Builders,
went to work under the direction of Doug Stout,
Construction Superintendent. He suggested to
Bishop Vigneron that a special blessing be held
before the first concrete was poured, asking protection for the workers. The workers then placed religious medals into the concrete as it was poured.

Webcor faced many construction challenges throughout the project. First, the unique design of the cathedral's support walls involved compound curves with two different radii, furthermore, leaning inward. Second, the framing of this totally innovative building had to be constructed literally from the top down.

First the excavation. On a sloping site, the plaza was designed to sit atop spaces for parking and for offices and gathering spaces. The site was excavated to place two levels of parking completely below grade. The cathedral itself rises over a crypt mausoleum at street level. Thus, the plaza and cathedral stand sixteen feet above Lake Merritt to the west, while adjoining with the neighboring buildings' plazas to the west.

By October 2005 the concrete was literally pouring in—eventually 120 million pounds of it, forming the lower levels and base of the center. At peak periods, up to 160 trucks were rolling onto the building site each day, pouring out their loads, and returning for more. Massive fifteen-foot-high walls form the base of the cathedral. A newly developed self-consolidating concrete that is stronger and more durable than previous types, and has a better finish and more attractive appearance, was used. Other buildings were starting to appear, such as the residence, cafe and gift shop.

This construction job was particularly dangerous because of its uniqueness . . . working on scaffoldings, hanging and dangling.

The concrete foundation wall is a thick and powerful support for the vaults above.

Doug Stout   Dan Burkett   Scott Wright

Cathedral-builders

Hundreds of workers have poured themselves into Christ the Light. They relish the unusual opportunity to create a sacred space, a historic structure. They have expressed themselves in wood and concrete and glass. Some of their names will be found by future generations, hidden in the ceiling. A few share their experiences in words, here.

Construction Superintendent Doug Stout continues a legacy of building. On his first job, in 1964, the construction superintendent was his father Roy. A proud member of the carpenter's union hall since then, Doug became one of the youngest superintendents by age thirty.

"Long before this project, I knew that building a cathedral would be very special," he acknowledges. "I had no idea I would close my construction career actually building one." During the project, Doug Stout read *Pillars of the Earth* by Ken Follett. This novel about the building of a medieval cathedral gave him "more understanding of the significance and spiritual dimension of what I'm building" and of the complex human dimensions of those involved, from bishops to laborers.

Dan Burkett and Scott Wright set out at 4:30 each morning from Modesto to work as carpenters on Christ the Light. "The size and scope of building something to last over 300 years got my attention," says Dan, who was on site from August 2005 to the completion.

With pride, the cathedral-builders will bring their children and grandchildren to see their work.

Invisible but essential, thirty-six huge, double-concave base isolators were in place by May 2006. Each one weighs 4000 pounds. Much infrastructure work done over the next year is nearly invisible in the completed building: slots in the floor that allow for passive heating and cooling as air rises, electrical work, plumbing.

By September 2006, an unusual framework ascended from inside the cathedral footprint: a 110-foot shoring tower. On the tower floor at the top, the fish-shaped oculus began to take shape. Within a month, a steel compression ring formed the oculus, allowing for the wooden ribs to be raised and bolted into place.

Twenty-six curved, 110-foot-long Douglas fir ribs, the trees that would shelter the sacred space, began to be assembled. Between the ribs, horizontal wooden louvers would filter the sun. They are progressively more open and angled to reveal the sky as they reach the top. In the chilly sunlight of early 2007, the wood glowed golden.

Douglas fir was also crafted into two ledges to support the organ pipes.

By July 2007, twenty-six straight mullions (also of Douglas fir), surrounded the inner vault. They supported aluminum frames that would hold the 1028 glass panels, each 10 feet by 4.5 feet. Within the double-layered glass, ceramic frits provided texture. By the end of

• • •

This tower rose to support an aerial construction platform.

Louvers between the beams are angled to allow more light to enter from the top.

• • •

the year, metal finials were in place above the structure, extending its height by eighteen feet. Craig Hartman has called them "architectural exclamation points."

Oakland was taking an interest, but the interior finishing was not visible to passersby, nor to the office workers in the Kaiser Center and surrounding buildings who had been watching the cathedral rise. If they were looking at the right time, they may have seen a crucial but almost comic moment.

The monumental image of Christ in majesty is so innovative that no one really knew whether its concept would work. Would light passing through the 94,000 pixels in the aluminum panels really create the desired effect? (See p.37.) Designers and manufacturers had been working in their studios, and at last mock-up panels arrived on site from Germany to be examined. Craig Hartman held his breath. A panel was lifted into place. The sun, however, shone onto the front of the panel, creating a dull impression. Webcor's Doug Stout knew what to do. He had a crane maneuvered to pick up a dumpster and hold it aloft, casting a shadow over the aluminum panel. Light could now be seen behind the panel, through the pixels. Lo! and behold— a portion of the face of Christ! The panels went into the Omega window in January and February 2008. The effect was magnificent.

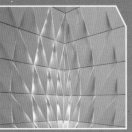

The Cathedral Center by the Numbers

- 2.5 acres
- room for 2000 on plaza
- 120 million tons of concrete
- 118' tall from plaza level to top of roof
- 18' finials projecting above the roof
- 26 curved Douglas fir ribs, 110' tall
- 26 straight Douglas fir mullions, 101' tall
- 768 louvers
- 1028 glass panels, 10'x4.5'
- 94,000 pixels in Omega window
- pixels from 1/8" to 1" in diameter
- seating for 1350
- 5,298 organ pipes
- 882 crypts and 1856 niches in mausoleum
- 500,000 Catholics in the Diocese of Oakland

This ledge will support organ pipes.

Meanwhile, artists sculpted and painted statues, Stations of the Cross, and a triptych. Fabricators crafted stone and metal into altar, baptismal font, ambo, cathedra, tabernacle, candle-holders, floor inscriptions, and cruci-fix. Restorers cleaned and refurbished stained glass, paintings and mosaics.

Everyone gave thanks for the safety of the workers, with no time lost to injuries.

By September 2008 the cathedral was ready to open its doors in welcome.

The metal finials add eighteen feet to the cathedral's height.

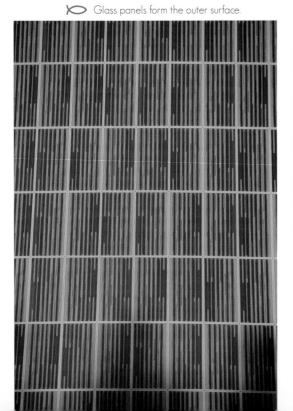

Glass panels form the outer surface.

Workers install the aluminum panels which make up the Omega Window's image of Christ in majesty.

Brother William Woeger, FSC, oversaw the liturgical design process.

The Cathedral's Sacred Art and Design Committee advised Brother William and Fr. Paul Minnihan (right) throughout planning and construction. Here the committee studies finishings of the cathedra.

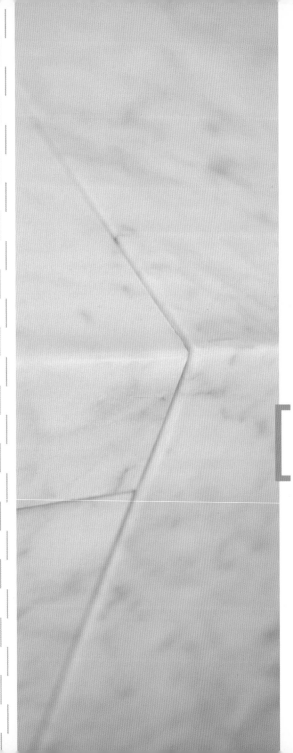

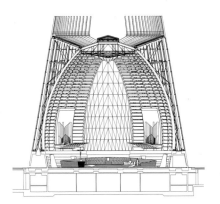

Creation and
Redemption

Alpha and Omega

"I am the Alpha and the Omega...." With
these words the voice of Christ proclaims his
identity in the Book of Revelation. As alpha begins the Greek alphabet and omega is its last
letter, Christ is the beginning and the end, and
he embraces all that falls between.

The cross above the cathedral entryway signals this focus on Christ with its imposing proportions (35'x 20').

The God who formed the universe has entered into human life and draws us into its eternal fulfillment. Jesus Christ was and is the key event of human history. Time flowed forward to his birth, life, death and resurrection. Time and grace carry humanity to a point out of time, where we will be one in him.

The cathedral manifests this profound and lofty faith. The building itself leads us along an axis from Creation to Redemption. Creation dances in the vitality of the Alpha window over the entryway. In lyrical patterns, the aluminum panels open to light, like leaves unfurling in springtime. At the other pole of this axis is the Omega window, with its magnificent image of Christ in majesty: truly human, truly divine.

Movement along this axis passes through the sacraments, from the baptistry to the altar. In Baptism the Christian enters into new life. This life reaches its climax in the Paschal Mystery, which Christ himself makes present in every Eucharist.

Above the entrance, a monumental cross expresses the cathedral's focus on Jesus Christ.

An Eye to the Heavens

Movement courses across the cathedral ceiling, which provides a transition from alpha to omega. Light enters through patterned aluminum panels in this skylight, or oculus (Latin for "eye"). And what dynamic patterns! Surging with energy, they emerge from the alpha window and pulse toward the omega window as toward a magnet.

The oculus illustrates the power recognized by the Jesuit scientist and theologian Pierre

• • •

 The oculus makes a powerful transition between alpha and omega.

••• Teilhard de Chardin (1881-1955). A paleontologist studying the earth itself, Teilhard was inspired by Saint Paul's vision of Christ as "the firstborn of all creation" (Colossians 1:15) to recognize Creation's evolution toward ever-greater oneness in Christ. Creation's goal, he saw, is Christ, the Omega Point, to whom the universe is drawn for its fulfillment in cosmic unity. The cathedral's energy moves in precisely this direction.

The conical outer walls end at the oculus, rather than closing the cone. The oculus opens the cathedral to the sky, which can be glimpsed through the panels.

The opening repeats the fish shape of the building's outline. Its rim acts as a compression ring, holding the vertical wooden ribs together. In a powerful tension, the ring resists the outward pull created by the two halves of the structure.

Christ, the Omega Point

Christ in majesty fills the Omega window. He is the Omega point, the goal of all Creation. In the words of Saint Paul, Christ is the one "in whom all things hold together...in [whom] all the fullness was pleased to dwell and through him to reconcile all things..." (Colossians 1:17-20).

The figure of Christ draws upon a masterpiece in the west façade of the cathedral of Chartres, France. This powerful portrayal shows a royal personage, coming at the end of time. The Second Coming of Christ is a standard element of Gothic cathedrals, ordinarily sculpted on the tympanum (triangular space) above the door in the central west portal. The position, facing the setting sun, suggests the end of this world, the conclusion of created realities. As carved on Romanesque cathedrals, such depictions often evoke fear of judgment, portraying Christ with wrathful features. Art historian Helen Gardner notes the difference between those older carvings and the relief sculpture on the west portal at Chartres. She describes the Chartres image as solemn, reflective, as one bringing salvation, not judgment. This is the prototype for Oakland's monumental image.

The Book of Revelation provides the scriptural source for a throne set in the heavens (Revelation 4:10). Ancient symbols manifest deep truths at Chartres and here in Oakland. Christ's seated posture, enthroned, is manifestly royal. While kings may not be common today, we recognize this way of expressing that Jesus Christ is the Lord of time and of all Christians. His followers look to him for guidance and protection. His right hand is raised in the traditional gesture of blessing. He comes to mediate God's blessing to every created being.

Just as traditional is the closed book in his left hand. Again, the Book of Revelation provides the interpretation (Revelation 5:5-9). The book contains God's plan for the world. Only the Lamb—Christ, sacrificed and triumphant—can open the book. Human history unfolds between its covers, between Genesis and Revelation. He, the eternal Word—Alpha and Omega—is its meaning.

Oakland's window translates Chartres' twelfth-century vision with twenty-first-century digital technology. It was a daring application. A computer-enhanced image of the sculpture was digitized in 94,000 pixels. These were transferred into perforations in aluminum panels. The pixels became tiny circles, with diameters ranging from 1/8" to 1". Light enters the perforations. The stunning result is the monumental portrayal of Christ in glory that forms the Omega window. In a breath-taking fusion of form and meaning, Christ emerges as light itself.

Baptistry and Creation

The Church's sacramental life moves along the axis between Creation and Redemption. Through Baptism comes new life. Through Baptism the Christian enters the Church, becoming a living member of Christ's body.

Appropriately located at the cathedral's entrance is the baptistry. An inscription defines the circular area with a reference to Genesis, set into the floor in stainless steel letters: "The Spirit of God hovered over the waters. And God said 'Let there be light' and there was light" (cf. Genesis 1:2-3). Here at the cathedral entrance, under the Alpha window which celebrates Creation, the New Creation begins for each person baptized here.

A circle, the most perfect form in nature, represents heaven in Asian art. In Western art it represents eternity. Both meanings reinforce the purpose of the baptistry.

The font holds the water that is poured over the new Christian, who is baptized "in the name of the Father and of the Son and of the Holy Spirit." Jet black granite conveys a sense of mysterious depth, the unseen but solid reality known by faith. It is a mystery of life and death and new life. The early Church spoke of Baptism as "dying" and then rising to life in Christ:

The baptismal font is made of jet mist granite.

Are you unaware that we who were
baptized into Christ Jesus
were baptized into his death?
We were indeed buried with him
through baptism unto death,
so that, just as Christ was
raised from the dead,
by the glory of the Father,
we too might have newness of life.

(Romans 6:3-4)

Close to the baptistry are other features of the Church's liturgical life, related to the sacrament of Baptism. The Paschal candle bears the marks of Jesus' wounds, recalling that to enter his life is also to share in his death. Each year at the Paschal Vigil on Holy Saturday night, a new Paschal candle is marked, blessed, and lighted to the chanted strains of "Jesus Christ is the Light of the world...a light no darkness can extinguish." Throughout the year its flame burns during Baptisms and funerals, representing this faith in new life and life eternal.

In an adjacent wall the ambry, a glass-enclosed case, holds vessels of holy oils: chrism, the oil of catechumens, and the oil of the sick. They are used in sacramental anointings such as preparation for Baptism, Confirmation, Anointing of the Sick, and Ordinations.

Each Holy Week, a special ceremony, the Chrism Mass, takes place in the cathedral. Participants gather from the entire diocese. The bishop blesses the oils which representatives then carry back to their home parishes. This sacred event underlines the cathedral's central role in diocesan liturgical life.

The ambry makes it clear that the cathedral itself is also a parish, with its own cycle of sacramental life, flowing from Baptism.

Reconciliation

On each side of the baptistry is a chapel dedicated to the sacrament of Reconciliation, also known as Penance or Confession. Catholic liturgy demonstrates a realistic awareness that we need continual conversion. We are not always faithful. Again and again we fail to live fully the Christ-life poured into us at Baptism. In sacramental Reconciliation we return to the source, seeking renewal.

Each Chapel of Reconciliation has an inscription in the floor. "Repent and believe in the Gospel" (Mark 1:15) challenges and invites. The Gospel (meaning "Good News") calls us to change our lives for the better. The other inscription, "Christ Jesus came...to save sinners" (1 Timothy 1:15), assures us that Jesus' love is the power to make that change; he is our liberator from sin.

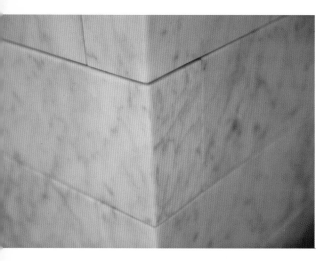

is a sacred meal. On the night before his death, Jesus celebrated the Jewish Passover with his closest followers. Giving thanks to God, he blessed bread, broke it and gave it to them, saying, "This is my body, which will be given for you; do this in memory of me"(Luke 22:19). He blessed wine and gave it to them to drink, saying "This cup is the new covenant in my blood, which will be shed for you" (Luke 22:20).

As a stone structure, the altar evokes the sacrificial stones of ancient Hebrew worship

The altar is made of Carrara marble.

This sleek, six-foot stainless steel candlestick, with a spun satin finish, is one of twelve. Six stand in the sanctuary, six in the mausoleum.

Altar and Redemption
· · · · · · · · · · · · · ·

The axis from Creation to Redemption moves from Baptism to Eucharist, from water to blood, from font to altar. The altar is the focal point of every Catholic church. Around it the community gathers to celebrate the Eucharist (from the Greek word meaning "thanksgiving"), the source and summit of Catholic worship. In this sacred action, Christ is present in the words of sacred Scripture and makes present once again his Last Supper and the sacrifice of his Pasch.

As a table, the altar recalls Jesus' final meal and reminds the community that the Eucharist

and the bare stone of Mount Calvary, where Jesus was crucified. The assembly shares in this sacrifice, offering God bread and wine which the Holy Spirit will transform into the Body and Blood of Christ. These natural elements represent the faithful, joined to Christ as his body in the Eucharistic sacrifice. He offered himself unto the pouring out of his blood on the Cross. He shares himself in Communion to nourish his body, the Church.

Now risen and ascended to heaven, Christ gathers us into redemption. He has freed humanity from slavery to sin by the power of his complete consecration to God, even to the point of death. With him we can "pass over" through death to eternal life: the Paschal Mystery.

Made of Carrara marble, the altar is natural and elemental. A cube set in the circle of the sanctuary platform, it evokes ancient Asian symbols for earth and heaven, respectively. Its symmetry—no front, no back—expresses the equality of all the baptized, gathered around the Lord's table. The altar sits on a cross-shaped surface within that circle (suggesting eternity). The Eucharist is a foretaste of eternal life.

 A communion cup crafted for the cathedral by Marirose Jelicich is seen against the background of the wooden reredos that embraces the sanctuary.

A Community at Prayer

Near the altar, the bishop's cathedra is situated within the seating for diocesan clergy. The wooden reredos separates the sanctuary from the Blessed Sacrament Chapel.

From very early times, Christians celebrated Eucharist in places made holy by the deaths and burials of martyrs. The prayer of the living was united with those whose lives and deaths had borne witness to the faith. Thus began the custom of including relics of the saints in altar stones, when churches began to be built.

The cathedral's altar too contains relics, inserted and sealed in the stone. The holy persons represented are Andrew, apostle; Thomas, apostle; Stephen, deacon and first Christian martyr; Sixtus II, pope from 257 to 258 and martyr; Perpetua, a young wife and new mother martyred in North Africa in 203; Cecilia, Roman martyr of the third century; early Christian martyrs Restituta and Speusippus; Francis of Assisi, founder of the Order of Friars Minor, the Franciscans (1181-1226); Colette of Corbie, Poor Clare who established many reformed monasteries (1381-1447); Francis de Sales, bishop and spiritual writer (1567-1622); Junipero Serra, Franciscan President of the California missions (1713-1784); John Vianney, parish priest (1786-1859); Pius X, pope who allowed children to receive Holy Communion (1835-1914). Two additional, unusual contents of the reliquary are soil from Auschwitz, commemorating the victims of the Holocaust (especially Saints Maximilian Kolbe and Teresa Benedicta [Edith] Stein) and a rock from Calvary.

The Christian community's continuity from generation to generation is called the Communion of the Saints. In another subtle reminder of this belief, glass-covered sections in the sanctuary floor allow light to pass into the mausoleum below, uniting the Church gathered around the altar with those who have gone before us.

The wooden reredos wall behind the altar encircles the sanctuary, which serves the community's prayer. The altar's elevation helps all who are present to see and experience their participation in the liturgy. Seating for clergy (presbyterium) can accommodate all the priests of the diocese. Red oak pews are ranged in curved ranks through the nave. Gathered around the altar, the presbyterium and the pews form a circle with seating that accommodates 1350.

At the center of the clergy seating is the bishop's jet black granite cathedra. Every cathedral takes its name from this official chair. It is a sign of the bishop's role as the diocese's chief pastor and teacher of faith. At his cathedra, the bishop presides over solemn liturgical functions such as conferring Holy Orders and blessing the chrism, in addition to Eucharistic celebrations.

Red oak pews are dappled with sunlight.

Music ministers—vocal and instrumental—close the circle. They occupy space designed to help them support the congregation's sung prayer. Their role is an integral part of the liturgy. Music unifies the participants, bringing them together in spirit and in action.

The organ was custom-designed and constructed by the firm of Orgues Létourneau. The console is close to the choir. At its keyboard the organist can play the choir and accompanimental divisions or the main organ. Dramatic architectural ledges were designed to hold the majority of the 5,298 pipes of this grand instrument.

A room behind the choir houses two divisions of pipes.

Within the sanctuary, the ambo stands as the privileged place for proclaiming God's word in Scripture. In this proclamation Christ, the Word, is present. The ambo, designed by Brother William Woeger, FSC, reflects this reality in an unusual feature: a crucifix. The bronze corpus (body) sculpted by Andrew Bonnette portrays a peaceful Jesus. Its serenity of posture and expression reflects classical influences, such as are also found in works of the Romanesque and early Medieval periods. The elongated arms stretch as though to embrace the world. Jefferson Tortorelli fashioned the red oak cross.

Jet black granite links the ambo with the baptismal font. Its position near the musicians' area links its ministry of the spoken word with the choir's ministry of the sung word.

Mary, Mother of the Church of Oakland

First among the faithful, as the Second Vatican Council called her, Jesus' mother Mary is honored with a statue in the sanctuary. Andrew Bonnette sculpted this cast-bronze representation of her as the principal patron of the diocese, "Mother of the Church of Oakland." Local elements that speak of this special relationship are the California oak sapling that shades her and the bear cub at her feet—symbols of the city and of the state.

The statue displays Mary's mission to bring Christ to the world. She brings her Child to us, offering us an opportunity to get to know him, to accept him as she has done.

The figure of Mary, Mother of the Church of Oakland (seen here in model form) is on the east side of the sanctuary.

Andrew Bonnette's bronze figure of Christ crucified is mounted on the ambo.

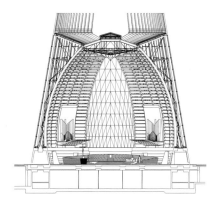

The Circle of
Devotion

Balancing the cathedral's lofty heights are its solid foundation walls. While the vaults leap to breath-taking theological insights, the ground-level devotional circuit touches hearts. Christ the Light invites us to both experiences, illuminating the whole person.

Way of the cross

I. Jesus is condemned to death.

II. Jesus takes up his cross.

III. Jesus falls for the first time.

IV. Jesus meets his mother.

V. Simon of Cyrene helps Jesus carry his cross.

VI. Veronica wipes Jesus' face.

VII. Jesus falls the second time.

VIII. Jesus meets the women of Jerusalem.

IX. Jesus falls the third time.

X. Jesus is stripped.

XI. Jesus is nailed to the cross.

XII. Jesus dies on the cross.

XIII. Jesus is taken down from the cross.

XIV. Jesus is laid in the tomb.

🐟 The Fourth Station: Jesus meets his mother Mary.

🐟 The Fifth Station: Simon of Cyrene helps Jesus carry his cross.

The Way of the Cross
. . . .

The Stations of the Cross which line the walls draw us into the Passion and death of Jesus. Andrew Bonnette's bronze sculptures trace Jesus' sufferings through biblical and traditional images. The sequence begins with Pilate delivering the death sentence and follows the route to Calvary, ending with the Crucifixion and burial.

The Way of the Cross includes fourteen Stations. For centuries, Christians have walked this devotional way in prayerful solidarity with their Savior. He accepted the vulnerability and humiliation that we experience. We walk with him and with his mother Mary, his friends, and his followers. We imagine ourselves called to assist him as was Simon of Cyrene. We think of the ways we can wipe his face, as did Veronica, by assisting the people suffering around us.

Bonnette's figures are elongated in a style reminiscent of Gothic sculpture. The intent is not realism but rather a spiritual and emotional impact that goes beyond the ordinary. If, as the saying goes, "The eyes are the windows of the soul," the enlarged eyes of these figures suggest a deep, soul-stirring experience. The suffering persons seem to look within and into eternity. We are invited to look with them.

Soft, indirect light gives the chapels a reflective atmosphere.

Devotional Chapels

In the embrace of the cathedral's foundation walls, a softer, muted light draws us into a series of chapels and into quiet, memories, reflection, and prayer. These chapels almost seem to be carved out of the thick walls, with skylights and small windows of different sizes and shapes admitting light. Flickering votive candles in amber-colored glass glow with warm light and symbolize the prayers of those who have lit them. The muted colors of the venetian plaster walls create a restful atmosphere.

Here, images speak to the heart, and beauty touches the spirit.

Catholic devotions express a faith that has struck root in a particular culture or ethnic group and therefore strengthen its identity. Yet devotions also grow out of universal human experiences such as family life or suffering or the seasons of the year and therefore can be shared. They integrate a cosmic faith and very human moments.

These chapels can be seen as satellites, revolving around Christ, the center.

The Chapel of the Holy Family

◁▷ St. Joseph holds the Child Jesus to extend a blessing upon the world, upon us.

The Chapel of the Holy Family communicates the power of loving relationships. The statues of Mary and of Saint Joseph with the Child Jesus radiate this energy with expressive gestures, smiles, and robes that flow or even dance. Luis Mora of Guadalajara, Mexico, carved the statues from cedar and applied the vivid colors that bring them to life and the precious stones that make them sparkle. The child in Saint Joseph's arms is both a happy baby reaching out to us and the Son welcoming us into God's embrace.

These contemporary statues and the other works of art in the chapel draw upon California's Latin American heritage. Paintings from the School of Cuzco, attributed to the studio of Diego Quispe Tito (ca. 1650) exemplify seventeenth-century Spanish colonial style.

The Return from Egypt conveys the same warmth that we see in the statues. The family members lean toward each other, mother and Son holding hands. An angel, unseen by them, makes us aware of God's protection. Warm, vivid colors suit the subject. Similar colors light up the scene of *The Adoration of the Shepherds*. The shepherds and the parents cluster in what the painter rendered as a circle with the divine Child as its center. The child Jesus is also the center of the composition in *The Circumcision of Christ*. Here he is the light illuminating the other figures. The darkness outside their circle suggests that the world needs his light. The traditional static, triangular composition of *Christ in the Temple* is broken by an unusual element: in the far left margin are Mary and Joseph, seeking Jesus. Their haloes of light suggest that they already hold him within.

The Chapel of the Suffering Christ

The cross in the Chapel of the Suffering Christ bears a nearly life-size corpus (Latin for body). This five-foot wooden sculpture is the work of a seventeenth-century Spanish Colonial artist. It shows the Crucified Jesus at the moment of his death. His body sags, his head has dropped to one side. His prominent ribcage almost suggests a skeleton, though the body is that of a healthy young man. The image looks squarely at the reality of death but also conveys the peace and trust of Jesus' final words, "Father, into your hands I commend my spirit."

In this chapel, a visitor can recognize that God's entry into human life was complete, unto the point of death. God's Son was not spared. God knows our sufferings from experience and accompanies us through them.

A seventeenth-century Spanish Colonial artist produced this image of Jesus crucified.

The T-shaped cross (often called *tau*, the Greek word for T) goes back to Saint Francis of Assisi and has a special place in Franciscan tradition. This element, as well as the origins of the sculpture, links the chapel with the Spanish missionary tradition that is so strong in California.

The Chapel of All Saints

The Chapel of All Saints is dedicated to those holy men and women of the past who have inspired particular devotion. Catholic tradition honors them on special feast days that punctuate the year. Images kept in this chapel will be moved into the main church for these annual celebrations.

Presiding over the chapel is a triptych honoring saints of particular importance to the Diocese of Oakland. Brother William Woeger, FSC, painted it on canvas. As his inspiration, Brother William drew upon an early Renaissance altar screen in the Capella Baroncelli in Santa Croce Church, Florence, Italy. The central panel honors Mary as Queen of the World. Under this title she is invoked as the principal patron saint of the diocese. On the right, Saint Joseph holds Mission San José. On the site of this mission, dedicated to him, Mass was first celebrated locally in 1797. The left panel

depicts Saint Francis de Sales holding the church dedicated to him, which served as Oakland's first cathedral from 1962 to 1989.

Chapel of the Seasons

The flow of time, with its journey of redemption, circulates through the Chapel of the Seasons. Each year the Catholic Church re-experiences God's saving action within Creation. Devotional images in this chapel are changed to mark the seasons of this cycle, e.g., the Nativity scene.

In Advent (December) the liturgical year begins with ardent longing for Christ's coming in time, in each heart, and in eternal fulfillment. This season culminates with Christmas (December 25) and with Epiphany (first Sunday of January). The Cathedral of Christ the Light celebrates Epiphany as its particular feast, marking the manifestation of Jesus as the Christ, not only to the Magi (Matthew 2) but to all peoples.

The season of Lent reminds us of Jesus' forty days of prayer and fasting in the desert at the beginning of his public ministry. Lent concludes with the Holy Week observances that focus on his Last Supper, Crucifixion and burial. This sequence, called the Paschal Mystery, explodes into Easter, celebrating his Resurrection from the dead and, forty days later, his Ascension into heaven.

Following Pentecost (fifty days after Easter), the season called "ordinary time" extends through November and culminates with homage to Christ in majesty on the feast of Christ the King.

These seasons are not merely remembrances but graced experiences of God's initiative on our behalf. Thus the chapel's threshold inscription is "You crown the year with your bounty" (Psalm 65:12).

Chapel of the Blessed Sacrament

In a chapel behind the cathedral's altar, the Blessed Sacrament is reserved. At every Mass, hosts of bread and wine are consecrated as the Body and Blood of Jesus Christ. After the Mass, some of the consecrated hosts are reserved in a place suited for private prayer. In the Cathedral of Christ the Light, this chapel is located directly behind the sanctuary, close to the altar and separated from it by the reredos wall.

The tabernacle which holds the Body of Christ is the focal point of the chapel but is also visible from the nave. Surrounded by the reredos wall, the tabernacle is made of stainless steel with bronze inlay. The bronze panels on the side facing the nave depict various images of gathering. The chapel side depicts the purposes for reserving the Blessed Sacrament: as medicine for the sick, food for the journey for those who are dying, adoration, and worship outside of the time of Mass. Brother William Woeger, FSC, designed and Andrew Bonnette sculpted the tabernacle.

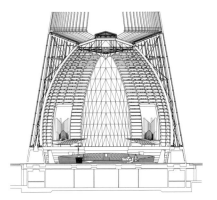

May They Rest ••• in Peace

Mausoleum

Ancestors in family, ancestors in faith.... The cathedral mausoleum bears witness to this continuity in the Church's great family of grace. Here we reverently lay to rest the remains of our loved ones. Though we say goodbye, our

relationship remains alive. Catholics use the term Communion of Saints to describe the belief that the living and the dead remain united. A striking feature of the mausoleum bears witness to this belief.

At the end of the long central aisle, below the sanctuary and altar, stands a white granite catafalque. Here the casket or urn is placed during the final prayers before entombment.

Light pours over it from above. These rays enter the mausoleum through glass panels in the sanctuary floor above. The light unites those who live with and in Christ, in heaven and on earth, the living and the dead.

The catafalque was crafted from the altar of St. Francis de Sales Cathedral. Laid here, the human body receives the respect due to that which has been a temple of the Holy Spirit and will rise again to life when Christ returns in glory.

Behind the catafalque, and beneath the Blessed Sacrament Chapel, are twelve crypts reserved for the bishops of the Diocese of Oakland. From very early times bishops have been buried in their cathedrals. The remains of Bishop Floyd Begin, Oakland's first bishop, have been transferred here.

Stained-glass windows beautify the crypt areas that radiate from the central aisle. These were imported from Germany for St. Francis de Sales Church. One window portrays Saint Francis de Sales as the patron saint of writers. Another shows Saint Patrick, apostle of Ireland, holding a church. The Apostles are represented with the symbols traditionally related to them, often the instrument of their martyrdom. In the Bishops' Crypt are stained-glass portrayals of Saints Peter and Paul. The window of Saint Peter displays a key, recalling Jesus' words, "I will give you the keys to the kingdom of heaven..." (Matthew 16:9). Saint Paul's sword represents his beheading and God's word, called a "two-edged sword" (Revelation 1:16).

Sharing the Light

No cathedral exists for itself alone, any more than the Church does. The leaders and supporters who built Christ the Light did so with a vision of openness, hospitality, and service. The plaza makes this dimension of cathedral life evident. It is urban, communal, linked to the city and to the ocean, even to the great Pacific Rim.

As their mother church, the cathedral gathers Catholics from the entire diocese—covering Alameda and Contra Costa counties—for ordinations to the priesthood and the diaconate, adult Confirmations, welcoming of new Catholics ("Rite of Election"), the Mass for the Blessing of the Holy Oils, celebrations of Catholic organizations and associations, gatherings from Catholic schools, and the annual ethnic diversity day, nourishing unity.

The cathedral center, offices, and other buildings on the cathedral campus also strengthen the diocesan mission. Far beyond the Catholic community, the cathedral seeks to be a welcoming place for believers, for our neighbors, and for visitors of all faiths and cultures. Through concerts and other artistic presentations, wisdom and goodness and beauty can be shared with others. As bearers of Christ's light in the East Bay, parishioners, pastors, and staff strive to gather good together.

In the tradition of St. Francis de Sales and St. Mary parishes, the cathedral seeks to model vibrant liturgies and outreach. Ministries of both evangelization and social service shed Christ's light in the central city. As part of the cathedral campus, the Order of Malta Oakland Clinic serves the uninsured poor through diagnostic care and referrals to providers of free healthcare. The plaza's Healing Garden is one part of a ministry to victim-survivors of clergy abuse.

Symbolizing the presence of the Catholic community in the East Bay, the cathedral represents the ongoing commitment which Christ calls this community to make to the city of Oakland and to all the cities and communities that surround it.